I0212394

A Butterfly asked Katie for a Story
by J. Fulkerson
© TXu002419969
ISBN 978-1-60307-331-8
Published by
Sarge Publications
866-878-2096
Printed in the U.S.A. by
Allegra Alpena
829 W. Chisholm Street
Alpena, Michigan 49707
www.allegraalpena.com

Katie Klondike did not like to read, it was hard for her. She was afraid that the other children would make fun of her if they heard her read.

One day a beautiful butterfly landed on Katie's shoulder and whispered, "Would you read me a story please? I have been traveling all day and I need a story to fall asleep."

Katie was afraid the butterfly would laugh at her and said, "I don't read very well." The butterfly said, "That's OK! You will get better with practice! I think I'll stay here in your warm sunny room for a while." The butterfly then flew to the fresh flowers Katie's had picked and lay down in a red flower.

Katie Klondike did not like to read, it was hard for her. She was afraid that the other children would make fun of her if they heard her read.

One day a beautiful butterfly landed on Katie's shoulder and whispered, "Would you read me a story please? I have been traveling all day and I need a story to fall asleep."

Katie was afraid the butterfly would laugh at her and said, "I don't read very well." The butterfly said, "That's OK! You will get better with practice! I think I'll stay here in your warm sunny room for a while." The butterfly then flew to the fresh flowers Katie's had picked and laid down in a red flower.

Priscilla Pendergrass likes to take photographs with her camera. Her favorite picture is one of yellow flowers. She thought the flowers were so petty that she put the picture in a frame and hung the frame on her wall.

Jesse Jacobs likes to read books about dragons and castles. He likes to pretend that he is a knight in shining armor that guards the kingdom.

Tamara Tibbles likes to make bookmarks on her computer. She made bookmarks that you can cut into four pieces. Then she would proudly give them to all her friends so everyone could find the last page they read.

Print the next page so have your own bookmark from Tamara!

read.
know.
grow.

read.
know.
grow.

read.
know.
grow.

read.
know.
grow.

Cut along the dotted lines to make 4 bookmarks

Read every day

Write everyday

Welcome to Mrs. Crabtree's Class

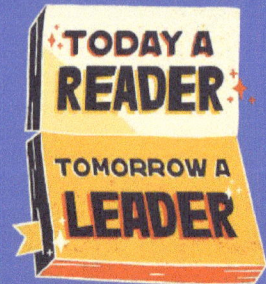

How Why ? whO What When Where

TODAY A READER TOMORROW A LEADER

All four students had met in Mrs. Crabtree's class.

At lunch, Tamara told Katie about the bookmarks she makes. Tamara told Katie that Mrs. Danco taught her to read better by writing happy sayings on them!

"Mrs. Danco taught me to read slower," said Tamara. That way I could sound out the words I didn't know. Going too fast makes us miss letter sounds. Did you know, Katie, that there are letters with more than one sound? They are called vowels!"

"They're the letters A, E, I, O, U and sometimes Y."

At lunch Jesse told Katie about the knights, castles, and dragons in his books. "Mrs. Danco taught me to read better by **telling** someone what story I read. When I **retell a story**, it helps me learn lots of new words and, I remember the story better too!" Jesse said.

The next day at lunch Priscilla told Katie about the stories she wrote about the pictures she took.

"Mrs. Danco told me I should use words I know to write my stories. Do you like to read stories?" Priscilla asked?

Katie said in a tiny, shy voice, "I love stories, but I don't read very well. Priscilla clapped and smiled very brightly. "Mrs. Danco will teach you how to read better, she almost shouted!"

Katie was so happy to learn there was a special teacher like Mrs. Danco. Katie really wanted to read better. She loved to listen to stories and learn new things.

Maybe I could learn to slow down when I read like Tamara said she does.

Maybe I could retell a story like Jesse said he does.

She knew she could use the words she knew to tell a story like Priscilla does with her pictures.

All four children were in Mrs. Crabtree's class when Mrs. Danco came into class with a big smile. "Excuse me Mrs. Crabtree, it's time for my reading helpers to come down to my room." Mrs. Danco said. Priscilla was first at the door and softly whispered in Mrs. Danco's ear. She said, "Our new friend Katie is afraid to read like we all were." Mrs. Danco thanked Priscilla, and walked to Mrs. Crabtree's desk. The teachers talked quietly for a couple minutes.

Mrs. Danco said in a soft voice, "Katie, could you come to Mrs. Crabtree's desk please?" Mrs. Danco leaned over and spoke softly to Katie, "I would like you to come to my reading class every day with your friends starting today. Would you like that?" Katie clapped her hands and almost shouted, "YES!" Smiling, Mrs. Danco said, "Well get in line and off we go.!"

When the bell rang at the end of the day, children filled the hallways heading to their buses. Katie sat in her normal bus seat and started daydreaming about reading a story to Ms. Butterfly. "I think I will call her Bonita, she thought."

The bus driver woke her from her daydream, "This your stop, young lady." She said. Katie walked to the front of the bus smiling. She was very excited about going to school tomorrow.

Katie kept thinking about what Priscilla, Tamara, and Jesse had told her about Mrs. Danco.

As soon as she got home, she ran upstairs and told Ms. Bonita Butterfly what happened at school.

SLOW
DOWN

Sound it out

In the morning Katie woke up excited. After getting ready for school, Katie went downstairs, grabbed an apple and yelled, "Bye Mom, I'm going to school!"

Once outside she skipped all the way to the bus stop.

As soon as Katie sat down in class, she started watching the clock. After a little time went by, Mrs. Danco came in and said, "Hi Mrs. Crabtree. I am here to pick up my reading helpers." "I'm here" said Katie and she lined up with Priscilla, Tamara, and Jessie.

Once in reading class, Tamara worked on writing new sayings for her bookmarks.

Jesse worked on writing new words to retell his stories about knights, castles and dragons.

Katie and Priscilla were elbow partners and Katie worked on reading out loud a whole page to Priscilla.

"You just have to write down the words you don't know. Once you write them down you learn new words really fast,"said Priscilla.

Sound it

SLOW DOWN

And so, Katie went to reading class every day for an hour with her friends. After about a week of practice writing new words and reading out loud Katie got better and better at knowing all the words in the stories she picked out. She picked out story's she hoped Miss Bonita would like.

HI Helpers, pick any book you want.

Write down five words you know and five words you don't know.

Once you have a list look up each word you do not know.

The write them down on flash cards.

Walking back to Mrs. Crabtree's class, Katie told her friends that she knew she was getting better at reading. Priscilla and Jesse clapped and said "That's great!" Tamara said, "I am so happy for you Katie." Katie was happy too and felt very proud of herself.

For three weeks, every day, the group of friends went down to Mrs. Danco's class. Katie could now read all the words on her flash cards without missing any. She was so happy that at the of Mrs. Danco's reading class, she gave Mrs. Danco the biggest hug and whispered with a big smile, "Thank you for helping me read better."

Mrs. Danco smiled and said something that Katie did not expect "You are ready to graduate from reading class! After tomorrow, you, Priscilla, every day. Just look at what you have learned.

You learned to *slow down when reading!*
You learned to *sound the word out!*
You learned how *vowels can have different sounds!*
You learned to *use new words you did not know!*
You learned to *retell a story with new and old words!*"

Mrs. Danco said, "You will come down tomorrow to review a what we learned. From now on you will be able to read and write new words all by yourself." Remember to ask you friends for help and Mrs. Crabtree and I are always here for you.

The next day all four friends received a certificate of achievement wrapped really fancy. Katie was both happy and sad. Then she remembered that Ms. Danco told her that she could come down and see her anytime she needed to. That made Katie feel much better.

As the children walked back to Mrs. Crabtree's class Katie said "I'm worried about what happens when the words get harder and harder?" Priscilla, Jesse, and Tamara just smiled at her. Tamara said, "Ms. Danco will help us every year to get better!"

Halfway to class Katie saw posters everywhere in the hall that other students had made. There were lots and lots of posters in the hallways. Katie was very surprised and whispered to the group as they walked to class, "U-mm-mmm" Said Katie," When did they hang all these posters?"

"Mrs. Danco said since now that we can read a lot more words, we recognize more sayings. That's how we know we are getting better at reading!" said Jesse.

Katie was looking at posters hanging in class, it seemed like a whole new classroom.

Later that day after lunch, Mrs. Crabtree asked for a volunteer to read the next four sentences from their workbook. Without thinking, Katie's hand shot up. Mrs. Crabtree smiled, her eyes bright and shining. "Thank you, Katie, please go ahead."

Great job finishing your book!

It is very important to remember that everyone learns differently so what helps you, might not be the same thing that helps someone else.

Can you answer these questions about what helped Tamara, Priscilla and Jesse's read better?

Write your answers below the questions

1. What did Tammy say helped her read better?

2. What did Priscilla say helped her read better?

3. What did Jesse say helped him read better?

4. Do you remember why Katie wanted to get better at reading?

Can you write to someone in your grade and retell the story with as many details as possible? Use a piece of loose leaf paper and do not worry about your penmanship too much. Remember Ms. Bonita said you will get better with practice!

1.

2.

3.

4.

5.

6.

www.ingramcontent.com/pod-product-compliance
Lightning Source LLC
Chambersburg PA
CBHW061051090426
42740CB00002B/117